THE POWER OF THE NIGHT

Peter Olaniran

THE POWER OF THE NIGHT

Copyright © 2022 by **Peter Olaniran**

PaperBack ISBN: 979-8-9869818-1-9

Printed in the United States of America. All rightsreserved solely by the author. This book or parts thereof may not be reproduced in any form, stored in a retrieval system, or transmitted in any form by any means—electronic, mechanical, photocopy.

Published by:

Cornerstone Publishing

A Division of Cornerstone Creativity Group LLC

Info@thecornerstonepublishers.com

www.thecornerstonepublishers.com

Author's Contact

To book the author to speak at your next event or to order bulk copies of this book, please, send email to:

polaniran@gmail.com

Contents

Dedication ii
Acknowledgments iii

1. Mysteries Of The Night 1
2. Mandates Of The Wicked 13
3. Mercies Of The Almighty 25
4. Miracles For The Redeemed 41
5. Mistakes Common To The Night Hours 55
6. Making Your Nights Victorious 67
7. Missiles Of Night Warriors 83

Dedication

To my loving wife, Olubunmi Yewande Olaniran, who has been standing by me; caring for me; loving me and providing support for me. I appreciate you, my good friend.

Also to my children (Joseph, Joshua, Michael, Daniel, Tosin and Noah) who have shown me love and support. I love you all so much.

Acknowledgments

I give thanks to the Almighty for the grace and inspiration to complete this book. I want to appreciate and give gratitude to my mentors: The General Superintendent – Christs Disciples Mission International, Rev (Dr) Olufemi Odubonojo and Pastor Esther Odubonojo, Late Rev (Dr) G.F Oyor. Thanks to the Almighty for your mentorship and guidance. And to my spiritual co-laborers of over 30 years; Pastors Afolarin and Adeola Abiona, Rev. Olufisayo and Moji Oderinwale, Pastor Olatubosun and Yewande Tubi, Pastor Yemi and Jadesola Onigbode, Pastor Wale (Late) and Tokunbo Mohammed; thank you for your encouragement and inspiration through our years of fellowshipping together.

I thank almighty God for the experience of life that inspired me. I am grateful to God for my children: Joseph, Joshua, Michael, Daniel, Tosin, and Noah, I love you all very much. I will also like to appreciate my CDMI family; and my CDMI Tower of Prayer family. You worth more than Rubbies and Gold to me. God bless you all.

In addition I will like to thank my Parents: Mr Napoleon and Mrs Bintu Olaniran (late) for their love and sacrifices. My wonderful aunties, Mrs Kehinde Yakubu and Mrs Taiwo Fashola who became my guardian. Thank you for your kindness. To all my siblings who the almighty has used to prepare me for the journey ahead Nathaniel Olaniran , Bukola Oni, Olabisi Oshodi (late) Gregory Olaniran , Yetunde Banjoko , Oyinade Olaniran; I love you all very much. May the Lord continue to be with us all.

Chapter 1

MYSTERIES OF THE NIGHT

"Desire not the night, when people are cut off in their place."

(Job 36:20)

As any astronomer or even the casual stargazer will readily affirm, nighttime offers a unique opportunity to behold some of the most amazing and awe-inspiring sights of the universe. From the twinkling stars and constellations, to the magnificent planets glowing beautifully like lamps, to the famous rings of Saturn, and the northern lights, waving ever so gently in celestial breeze - there is just so much to capture the eyes and astound the mind. So appealing and enthralling are these sights that people, right from ancient times, have always devoted a significant portion of their nighttime watching, observing and admiring the grandeur of the night sky with profound awe.

What most of these stargazers may not be aware of,

however, is that while they are busy marveling at these celestial wonders, something really horrible and disturbing is going in the same skies, which even the most powerful of telescopes on earth can never capture. A vast multitude of beings (legions upon legions of them), which occupy a portion of the skies called "the second heaven" are peering down into the earth and viciously engaged in monitoring, manipulating, contaminating, hijacking, diverting and distorting the destinies of individuals, families communities and nations. These are they which are described in the various Scriptural versions of Ephesians 2:2 as "power of the air" (KJV), "kingdom of the air" (NIV), "powers in space" (GNT), and "powers in the unseen world" (NLT). For certain reasons, which will be explaining shortly, nighttime offers the best opportunity for these wicked forces to execute their evil agendas on humanity.

Meanwhile, over here on earth, a similar scenario is unfolding. With the arrival of night and darkness, certain creatures commence their activities for the day – or more appropriately, for the night. In the terrestrial realm, certain animals, known as nocturnal animals, begin their hunt for preys to satisfy their hunger. You may already know some of such - hedgehogs, foxes, owls, aardvarks, and so forth. Oceanographers, too, have revealed that nighttime triggers the emergence of some uncommon marine creatures (the jumbo squid, for instance) on the ocean's surface, all in search of preys that will be so easy to catch at that hour.

Now, as you definitely must have observed or even

experienced in the course of your life, a certain group of human beings are not left out of this affinity with the darkness of the night. In fact, nighttime is what they crave the most. They love the night because they think it provides a good cover for their criminal and destructive activities. Job 24:13-16 describes them thus: "There are those who rebel against the light; they do not know its ways nor abide in its paths. The murderer rises with the light; he kills the poor and needy; and in the night he is like a thief. The eye of the adulterer waits for the twilight, Saying, 'No eye will see me'; And he disguises his face. In the dark they break into houses which they marked for themselves in the daytime; they do not know the light."

The message here is that evildoers, even among humanity, prefer the hours of the night than the day. Darkness inspires, empowers, emboldens and drives them into such depths of depravity and brutality that shatters the imagination of any right thinking individual.

The Disturbing Angle

But, then, if the dangers that confront humanity at night were to be limited to just these depraved and dangerous men and women, it definitely would have been a bit tolerable. All we would need to do would be to stay safely in our homes and ensure that our gates and doors are carefully locked and secured with security gadgets, while we trust the law enforcement agencies patrolling the streets to keep these godless souls at bay.

Unfortunately, there is a more frightening aspect of the night that all of the security gadgets and agencies in the world can never contend with. There are supernatural forces and powers that roam the world and our communities at night, who, together with their human agents, exploit the peculiarities of the night to unleash sorrows, pains, calamities, miseries, misfortunes, devastations and all sorts of perversion on mankind. Their sole mission as they comb the nook and corners of the earth is to steal, to kill and to destroy. And get this - their target is you and me, and the rest of mankind. As the Scripture says, "For we do not wrestle against flesh and blood, but against principalities, against powers, against the rulers of the darkness of this age, against spiritual hosts of wickedness in the heavenly places." (Ephesians 6:12).

Three important truths are contained in the above scripture that require your utmost attention. One, as already emphasized, the real enemies of your night are not the ones having flesh and blood. They are not the revelers, the burglars or the carjackers. These are dangerous, no doubt, but they can be easily contained with a few precautions. The ones that are more dangerous are the demonic agents and forces that are known as principalities, powers, the rulers of the darkness of this world and the spiritual wickedness in high places.

The second truth is that the darkness you see at night is much more than a natural or atmospheric phenomenon. That darkness is a kingdom on its own

– a kingdom with rulers, who dominate it and take advantage of the sleeping state of most humans to wreak havoc. So, have it in mind that the arrival of nightfall does not necessarily connote a general cessation or even relaxation of activities in your community. What you call the dusk or night, is actually the dawn of another kingdom; it is the beginning of frantic activities for the kingdom of darkness.

I once had an experience that gave me an insight into the fact that nighttime is not as peaceful in our world as most of us tend to see it. In 1998 when I ran a branch of our local church, I decided to visit the rented building where we would normally have fellowship and, to my surprise, strange things were happening there at night and I never knew. To my surprise, I discovered certain cult practices took place on Fridays nights every month around the same building. I was a local pastor and had no idea that this happened. This further opened my eyes to the need for vigilance and alertness. There are powers that can only operate at night. And it is my prayer that, as God brings you to the understanding of the power of the night, the story of your life, ministry, home, career, and children will change in Jesus' name.

The third revelation from the above verse is that these forces are extremely wicked, so much that they have become wickedness personified. In fact, the Scripture minces no word in letting us know that "the dark places of the earth are full of the habitations of cruelty" (Psalm 74:20, KJV). The primary occupations of these forces in their habitations or covens is to waste lives, abort destinies, delay breakthroughs, reverse miracle, truncate glories, terminate peace and poison joys. They are responsible for most of the attacks, setbacks, afflictions, infirmities, dysfunctions, crises and catastrophes that are experienced by individuals, families, communities, churches and nations.

Since no natural weapon, secular wisdom or human security infrastructure can defend us from the ruthlessness of these forces, what the Lord is about to reveal to us here, through His Word, are the supernatural weapons and strategies with which we must prevail over these night raiders. "For though we walk in the flesh, we do not war after the flesh: (For the weapons of our warfare are not carnal, but mighty through God to the pulling down of strong holds;) Casting down imaginations, and every high thing that exalteth itself against the knowledge of God, and bringing into captivity every thought to the obedience of Christ" (2 Corinthians 10:3-5).

God has designed His word to edify us and the Spirit of revelation to guide us. When individual believers or the church as a whole lacks information, then we end up as victims, like the rest of mankind. The difference between Christians and others is the level of information and revelation we carry. Lack of information can lead to serious deformation. This is why we must learn and master the strategies for victory over the forces of evil, especially the powers of darkness. If the kingdom of darkness is prepared to do what it takes to perform evil actions, then as Christians we must be willing to do whatever it takes to gain strength and power over these forces.

The Powers of Darkness

So, who exactly are these powers of darkness? They are the legions of demons, who together with Satan, their master, are on a lifetime mission of waging war against humanity, with the goals of derailing every individual from the will of God, perverting and diverting their destinies, subjecting them to perpetual bondage, and ultimately sinking their souls in everlasting destruction.

You will have a better understanding of the powers we are dealing with and why they are so brutal when you understand their origins. Revelation 12:3-9,12 gives us an interesting insight: "And another sign appeared in heaven: behold, a great, fiery red dragon having seven heads and ten horns, and seven diadems on his heads. His tail drew a third of the stars of heaven and threw them to the earth. And the dragon stood before the woman who was ready to give birth, to devour her Child as soon as it was born. She bore a male Child who was to rule all nations with a rod of iron. And her Child was caught up to God and His throne. Then the woman fled into the wilderness, where she has a place prepared by God, that they should feed her there one thousand two hundred and sixty days. And war broke out in heaven: Michael and his angels fought with the dragon; and the dragon and his angels fought, but they did not prevail, nor was a place found for them in heaven any longer. So the great dragon was cast out, that serpent of old, called the Devil and Satan, who deceives the whole world; he was cast to the earth, and his angels were cast out with him… Therefore rejoice, O heavens, and you who dwell in them! Woe to the inhabitants of the earth and the sea! For the devil has come down to you, having great wrath, because he knows that he has a short time."

We understand from this passage that, first of all, when Satan rebelled against God, he equally influenced and corrupted one-third of the angels of heaven ("the third part of the stars of heaven"). These are the demonic forces who assist the devil in accomplishing his missions. Secondly, we understand that we can never experience the lasting peace and rest we crave for, except we are ready to wage war. We are told that there was war even in heaven, with the devil and his demons fighting vehemently to usurp the throne of God, until they were defeated and disgraced out of heaven. If the angels of God had to fight to ensure that the heavenly order was preserved, we cannot do less, if we want the will of God to be established and sustained in our lives, families, churches, communities and nations.

Thirdly and most importantly, for our present discussion, we know that the earth in which mankind currently inhabits is no longer the peaceful Garden of Eden, but a battle arena, where the devil and his legions of demons, have come to transfer aggressions arising from their humiliating defeat in heaven. These powers have come against us "with great wrath". I pray you don't become one of their victims, in the mighty name of Jesus.

Reality of Spiritual Warfare

I have given you the above background to let you understand that, regardless of the luxuries, beauties, riches and pleasures you may see all around, the earth is not a playground but a battleground. Whether you know it or not, behind everything you see is an ongoing war against your soul, peace, joy, freedom, productively, prosperity and destiny. The devil and his demons, as well as their human agents (whom they possess to become witches, wizards, corrupters, persecutors and oppressors) are constantly unleashing their wicked agendas against humanity through every available means.

As Pedro Okoro, author of *Crushing the Devil* says, "Spiritual warfare is very real. There is a furious, fierce, and ferocious battle raging in the realm of the spirit between the forces of God and the forces of evil. Warfare happens every day, all the time. Whether you believe it or not, you are in a battlefield. You are in warfare."

Being in such a combat zone requires being adequately aware, armed and alert at all times, so we are not caught off-guard and become victims. "Lest Satan should get an advantage of us: for we are not ignorant of his devices" (2 Corinthians 2:11). The devil, his demons and his human agents are everywhere and in different forms — on the streets, in the media, in the music and movies industry, as well as in the fashion industry. This is why we are severally warned in the Scripture to be very careful how we live (Ephesians 5:15); to put on the whole armor of God (Ephesians 6:11); to prepare our minds for action (1 Peter 1:13); to make every effort (2 Peter 1:5); to and to be self-controlled and alert (1 Peter 5:8).

In the words of Dr. Edward Welch, the above admonitions are "are battle cries, and Scripture is full of them…you are not always sure where the enemy lurks. It is guerrilla warfare. There are strategically placed snipers. You let down your guard for a moment and the village you thought was safe suddenly opens fire on you."

I pray you will be wise.

Prayer Points

1. Thank you, Lord, for the revelation you have given me concerning the mysteries of the night and the reality of warfare.

2. I declare, in the name of Jesus, that I will not be ignorant of the devices of the devil, in the name of Jesus.

3. I declare that I shall not be consumed by the evils of the night in the name of Jesus.

4. I fortify my life, home, business, career and ministry with the blood of Jesus.

5. I receive the immunity of the Holy Spirit against demonic attacks of the night, in the name of Jesus.

Chapter 2

MANDATES OF THE WICKED

"The enemy said, 'I will pursue, I will overtake, I will divide the spoil; My desire shall be satisfied on them. I will draw my sword,
My hand shall destroy them.'"

(Exodus 15:9)

So far, we have not fully answered the crucial questions of why humanity should be the target of the devil's attacks and why the night seems to be so attractive to the demonic kingdom to launch their attacks against mankind. Let's quickly do so.

As you may already know, mankind is the crown of God's creation on earth. In fact, to him was initially given the control of the earth. Unfortunately, the devil, who was once a prominent angel of God and was then known as Lucifer, has always been uncomfortable with the exalted position and authority given to man.

Indeed, as several inspired Bible scholars have noted, the creation of man actually contributed to the ultimate rebellion of Lucifer against God, as he felt slighted not to have been consulted before the creation.

You can then easily understand why, immediately after his expulsion from heaven, as we saw in the previous chapter, the next target of the devil became humanity and the purpose of God on earth. He must have reasoned that if he could not manipulate and distort the purpose of God in heaven, he could as well try his treachery with the same humanity that he had never been happy with. This was why the angels proclaimed immediately after the defeat of the satanic hordes: "Therefore rejoice, O heavens, and you who dwell in them! Woe to the inhabitants of the earth and the sea! For the devil has come down to you, having great wrath, because he knows that he has a short time." (Revelation 12:12).

The Fatal Fall

Sadly, it was at this point that the vulnerability of mankind to demonic afflictions and oppressions began. Recall that soon after God created and blessed man, He told man that the key to his uninterrupted power, dominion and authority over the earth was his continued connection to the Almighty through obedience. God clearly told him, "Of every tree of the garden you may freely eat; but of the tree of the knowledge of good and evil you shall not eat, for in the day that you eat of it you[a] shall surely die." (Genesis 2:16-17)

Well, you already know what happened. Satan, who knew the secret of man's dominion and wanted to spite God, subtly deceived man by presenting falsehood to him. Not knowing what was at stake, man fell and the tables immediately turned against him and in favor of his vicious enemy.

So, you have a full picture of what humanity has to contend with in a few words: Man's original power derived from his connection to God. Satan and his demons had always hated and envied man. Satan sought for an opportunity to relegate man and accomplish on earth what he couldn't accomplish in heaven. Man willingly chose to heed the voice of the devil and consequently disconnected himself from God. The devil, seeing that man's source of glory and strength was gone, took over his place and from then began to execute his agenda of enslaving, humiliating and tormenting mankind – which ultimately is a way of getting back at God. Put simply, it gladdens the heart of the devil and his agents to reduce man to nothing and waste his destiny. But my prayer is that your life and destiny will not be wasted in the name of Jesus.

Thank God for the coming of the Lord Jesus Christ. With his finished work at Calvary, anyone who accepts Him can break the yoke and dominion of Satan and his agents over his life. 1 John 3:8 says, "…For this purpose the Son of God was manifested, that he might destroy the works of the devil." I declare every work of the devil destroyed in life, in Jesus' name.

We will explore this better in later chapter. But for now, let's consider another crucial aspect of this chapter.

Snare of the Night

So, why is the satanic kingdom more active and dangerous at night? Well, the first truth you must recall is that the predominant agenda of the devil has always been to counter the purpose of God. God had created both the day and the night for the good of mankind. The day is when man is empowered to be fully active – spirit, soul and body. This makes him less susceptible to attacks.

The night is when God designed for man to rest and be rejuvenated. Thus, God made the night and the accompanying darkness to have a lulling effect on man. Moreover, it is at night that man can easily and consistently be in that phase of sleep known in scientific parlance as REM (Rapid eye movement). It is the time when some essential and uncommon body functions can occur. During this REM or deep sleep phase, our breathing, heartbeat, body temperature, and brain waves reach their lowest levels; our muscles are extremely relaxed, and we are most difficult to rouse. God purposely designed it this way, so that He, the Almighty, can accomplish some amazing purposes in our lives and in our environment, without our interference. We will see some of these purposes in the next chapter.

Now, since the devil passionately hates man and opposes God, he has decided that the same night, especially in the thickest of darkness and deepest of sleep, when man has become extremely vulnerable, is when he and his agents will employ to perpetuate their evils. This is a normal strategy, even in military warfare. Sun Tsu, the legendary war strategist, says of facing an enemy in warfare, "Attack him where he is unprepared, appear where you are not expected."

The proof of the perversion of the night and man's extreme vulnerability to the wiles of the demonic kingdom at this time is confirmed in Job 36:20, where the Scripture says: "Desire not the night, when people are cut off in their place." In other words, the same night that God had purposed for the good of man has been infiltrated by his enemy to become the epicenter of attacks against him. It is for this reason that C.H. Spurgeon counsels, "When thou sleepest, think that thou art resting on the battlefield; when thou walkest, suspect an ambush in every hedge."

Make no mistake about it – nighttime has become an avenue of cruelty against humanity by the forces of hell. And you must also be aware that there is a significant reason why these forces are called powers of darkness or rulers of darkness. While it is true that they can be active in the day, they are much more active, powerful and brutal in the night. It is in the same way that the dawn brings a renewal of strength and energy for productivity for mankind that the night fills the demonic kingdom with a frenzied zeal for affliction and destruction upon the human race. I pray, once again, that you will not become one of their preys in the name of Jesus.

Specific Dangers of the Night

So, what exactly do the powers of darkness unleash on humanity at night?

1. Implantation of crises, calamities and contaminations

Note this very carefully. The spiritual controls the physical. Most of the crises and calamities, failures and setbacks that come upon individuals, families, churches, communities and nations are as a result of demonic activities in the spiritual realm at night.

The thoughts of God for our lives are thoughts of peace and not of evil. He says He desires for us to prosper and be in health, just as our souls prosper (3 John 2). So, how do sorrows, misfortunes, repeated disappointments, unexplainable hardship and sudden reversal of fortunes and blessings get into our lives, homes, ministries, businesses, finances and communities? Here is the answer in Matthew 13:24-28: "Another parable He put forth to them, saying: "The kingdom of heaven is like a man who sowed good seed in his field; ^{25} but while men slept, his enemy came and sowed tares among the wheat and went his way. ^{26} But when the grain had sprouted and produced a crop, then the tares also appeared. ^{27} So the servants of the owner came and said to him, 'Sir, did you not sow good seed in your field? How then does it have tares?' ²⁸ He said to them, 'An enemy has done this…'"

Tares are injurious weeds that have the appearance of good plants. They primarily damage plants' growth and ability to produce healthy crops, while also irritating. This exactly is what the enemy has done and he is still doing in many lives, homes and ministries today. People are facing all sorts of battles, rejections, oppositions, confusions, misunderstandings and downturns that they cannot explain the origin. Dear friend, an enemy has done this. But my prayer for you is that the Lord Almighty will fight for you and deliver you from every satanic implantation in the name of Jesus. I declare upon you that everything that God has not planted in your life, home, business, ministry, or career be uprooted by fire in Jesus' name.

2. Exchange of destiny

The life that many are living now and the yokes they are bearing in their lives are not theirs. A demonic exchange has taken place in their lives that must be reversed. And it is my prayer for you that the Lord will surely turn your situation around and undo every satanic exchange in your life, in Jesus' name.

Here is the biblical account of an evil exchange in the night: "Then came there two women, that were harlots, unto the king, and stood before him. And the one woman said, O my lord, I and this woman dwell in one house; and I was delivered of a child with her in the house. And it came to pass the third day after that I was delivered, that this woman was delivered also: and we were together; there was no stranger with us in the house, save we two in the house. And this woman's child died in the night; because she overlaid it. And she arose at midnight, and took my son from beside me, while thine handmaid slept, and laid it in her bosom, and laid her dead child in my bosom." (1 Kings 3:16-20).

What a wicked world in which we live! But for the vigilance of the woman with the living child, the enemy's plan for her was to turn her joy to sorrow, her testimony to tears and her dreams to a mirage. This is the same agenda of the demonic kingdom for humanity. And sadly, they have been succeeding in the lives of many people. The reason a good number of people are not able to fulfil their potentials, with many terminating their own lives over repeated failures, is not because they are not hardworking enough; the reason is that the enemy has hijacked their glory and destiny; and all of their efforts to succeed and breakthrough have become like flogging a dead horse. May you not labor in vain, in the name of Jesus. May the devil not turn your joy into sorrow, in Jesus name!

3. Terrors and pestilences

Nighttime is generally the time that the forces of darkness unleash terrors on mankind, especially through frightening oppressions and nightmares. The

Scripture confirms this, saying, "Thou shalt not be afraid for the terror by night…nor for the pestilence that walketh in darkness" (Psalms 91:5-6).

Terrors here refer to the various ways (sights and sounds) with which the powers of darkness enslave the individual in the bondage of fear. The Bible indeed mentions that a crucial part of Jesus' mission on earth was to "deliver them who through fear of death were all their lifetime subject to bondage" (Hebrews 2:15). One of the ways the powers of darkness torment mankind and perpetuate this bondage is through manipulations of dreams or causing recurrent nightmares. There are many people who find it difficult to sleep from night to night out of fear of what will happen once they close their eyes

But there is an even more sinister part. The Scripture talks about the pestilence or disease that casually strolls or stalks in darkness. In other words, nighttime is a time when demonic pestilences (diseases) move freely among humans. It is a time when the demonic kingdom releases the seeds of sicknesses and infirmities into the bodies of human beings. This is such a common phenomenon. How many times have people slept healthy only to wake up with symptoms of diseases, some which have turned out to be debilitating or even incurable?

Sometimes people sleep, hale and hearty, and wake up paralyzed, blind or even mentally deranged. The dark places of the earth are indeed the habitations of cruelty!

4. Deadly oppressions, intimacy and bloodsucking

This is another terrible dimension of the activities of the powers of darkness at night. There have been several individual accounts from people who said they found themselves incapacitated at night by a mysterious being that infiltrates their bed-space and pins them down, rendering them powerless, voiceless and immobile – until the intruder has accomplished its mission of robbing them of their glory.

But things can get even more serious. There are demonic forces that subject people into forced sexual intimacy in the night, thereby subjecting them to a perpetual covenant of bondage, failures and setbacks, especially at the edge of success. And of course, there are some of the wicked spirits who force their victims to eat all manners of dangerous things while asleep in other to dominate and manipulate their spirit, as well as poisoning their body system.

Moreover, since blood is known to have rejuvenating powers in the spiritual realm, some demons suck the blood of people through diverse means. This often occurs in the dream world, but surprisingly, some demons directly suck the blood of their victims by physically subduing them before drawing off their blood and thereafter leaving them not only physically exhausted but also spiritually exposed to all sorts of miseries and misfortunes. Indeed, for some people, such encounters often happen when they are about to have a breakthrough – after which, all their expectations are dashed and they find themselves in the depths of failure and crisis again.

May the Spirit of God crush the mouth of every power sucking away your blessings, glory, peace, joy and progress, in the name of Jesus.

5. Sudden premature death

This is the climax of the evils of the night. Since it is very difficult for demonic forces to operate fully in the physical, they patiently wait for the hours of the night when they have unfettered access to the spirit of man and then launch their attack – knowing full well, that once the spirit is finished, every other part will be finished.

Sadly, these attacks can sometimes involve the termination of a life altogether. All they need is to cut off, through a violent attack, the thin cord that connects the spirit to the body, such that the spirit that is fully active in the spirit realm is never able to return fully to the body and the person will be pronounced dead. This happens on a daily basis in our world – people sleeping and ascending the into the spirit realm, without being able to ever return again. May this never be your portion, in Jesus' name.

Prayer Points

1. Father in heaven, I thank you for exposing the mandates of the satanic kingdom to me.

2. I declare in the name of Jesus that the mandates of the wicked shall never be fulfilled upon my life, family, career, ministry and finances, in the name of Jesus.

3. I decree a divine recovery and restoration of every demonic exchange in my life and my household in the name of Jesus.

4. I reject, by fire, every demonic deposit in my household and ministry in the name of Jesus.

5. I nullify with the blood of Jesus every handwriting of calamity, setback, accident, failure and premature death over my life, family and ministry, in the name of Jesus.

Chapter 3

MERCIES OF THE ALMIGHTY

"It is of the LORD's mercies that we are not consumed, because his compassions fail not. They are new every morning: great is thy faithfulness."

(Lamentations 3:22-23)

I believe that with the amounts of revelation we have received regarding the menace of the night and the mandates of the satanic kingdom upon humanity, certain questions may have started to trouble your mind. For instance, if these forces of darkness are so many and so ruthless in their daily activities, why haven't they succeeded in wiping off or even subjecting the whole of humanity to sicknesses and afflictions? If the night is so full of evil, why do we still have to sleep at night? And why can't God just scrap the night altogether, since it has become the enclave of evil powers? These are crucial questions that will form the focus of our attention here, and it is my prayer that, in unraveling the answers, the Holy Spirit will further open your eyes of understanding and catapult you to greater dimensions of power and dominion, especially in your nightly hours.

Two crucial factors are at work here – the **mercy** and the **sovereignty** of God. You see, God is extremely merciful to humanity in general and to His children in particular. Despite the fact that we willingly sold ourselves to the satanic kingdom and consequently made ourselves vulnerable to their wickedness, God still cares for us and thus tempers the activities of the wicked against us. This explains why the devil and his demons cannot just unleash total destruction on the whole of humanity, even in the hours of the night.

Indeed, it was the wonder of this unfathomable love and care of God for humanity that overwhelmed the Psalmist in Psalm 8, so much that he declared: "What is man that You are mindful of him, And the son of man that You visit him? For You have made him a little lower than the angels, And You have crowned him with glory and honor. You have made him to have dominion over the works of Your hands; You have put all things under his feet, All sheep and oxen—Even the beasts of the field, The birds of the air, And the fish of the sea that pass through the paths of the seas. O LORD, our Lord, How excellent is Your name in all the earth!" (Psalms 8:4-9).

As I already noted, the demonstration of this mercy of God is manifested to the entirety of mankind.

But for God's children, He specifically watches over us and fights for us - which brings about mighty interventions, miracles and breakthroughs in our lives and circumstances. We will explore the various aspects of this move of God in defense of His children in the next chapter. And, as we will also see, God often needs our involvement to execute many of these special interventions and if we cooperate with Him, we shall continually prevail.

Unlimited Sovereignty

The more important factor here however is the SOVEREIGNTY of God. That word is powerful and should give you great assurance, especially as a believer. Regardless of the frequency and fierceness of the activities of demonic forces in our world, the Lord Almighty remains the supreme ruler of the entire universe, including the earth; and He is still the undisputed Lord and King over the affairs of mankind. Psalm 97:1 says, "The Lord reigns; Let the earth rejoice; Let the multitude of isles be glad!"

So, while it is true that man relinquished his dominion on earth to the devil and his demons, God has never and will never cede His supremacy over the whole of creation to any power or force. He is still ever in control – which means that, as we seek His move, He can decide to intervene and overrule the imaginations and devices of the wicked forces, especially for the sake of His children. Job 5:12 says that "He frustrates the devices of the crafty, so that their hands cannot carry out their plans."

Specifically for the night, there is another dimension of this sovereignty that I will be dwelling upon for the rest of this chapter. I mentioned previously that God created the night to achieve some beautiful purposes in the life of man and in the whole of nature. This is why nighttime can never cease on earth. In fact, while making a covenant with Noah and the rest of humanity, God has categorically declared: "While the earth remains, Seedtime and harvest, Cold and heat, Winter and summer, And day and night Shall not cease" (Genesis 8:22).

You can understand then that the night persists because God's purpose for it and in it continues undisturbed. This, again, confirms the immutable authority of God over His works, including the hours of the night. The Scripture, in fact, declares that God has not given over the night to the forces of darkness. It says, "The day is yours, the night also" (Psalm 74:16). Therefore, being the handiwork of God, designed for the benefit of humanity, nighttime harbors some uncommon, divinely-imputed qualities that we must learn to harness and maximize to our advantage. These include:

1. **Physical healing and rejuvenation**

Even with the machinations of the enemy, the desire of God for man to rest at the end of each day's activities hasn't changed. And there is a powerful purpose for this, which even science clearly confirms. Night sleep has healing and rejuvenating power for the cells, tissues and organs of the human body. In other words, night sleep has been designed by God to act as "nurse for tired nature."

It is in the course of the night that God causes your body to be revitalized and prepared for the productivity of the next day. Without this nightly rejuvenation, so many things can go wrong. As A.W. Pink rightly says, night sleep "is indeed a *merciful provision* of God's, which none of us appreciate as highly as we should." You will understand the truth in this statement when you realize that God has embedded in night sleep certain renewing capabilities that cannot be achieved any other time of the day.

Consider, for instance, the REM phase of sleep, which I mentioned in the previous chapter. God has designed it such that it is at this point that He carries out some surgical and therapeutic works upon our body. Remember that when God wanted to work on the body of Adam to form Eve, He had to first cause him to enter into this deep sleep. These same merciful works have continued to be carried out on us by God at night. As even science can confirm, while we're sleeping, our brain and body don't just shut down. Internal organs and processes are hard at work throughout the night. According to *Healthline*, it is during night sleep that "tissue growth and repair take place, important hormones are released to do their jobs, and cellular energy is restored."

In addition to this, your brain and mind too receive some supernatural touch of God's unfailing mercies.

During the night, your memories are consolidated, your blood sugar levels and metabolism balance out, your mood is stabilized, your immune system is energized and your brain detoxifies.

What this means, in a nutshell, is that the night is imbued with healing and regenerative powers. Therefore, I pray for you in the name of Jesus, that every hurt, affliction, disappointment and frustration that may have happened in your life will suddenly vanish within the hours of the night in Jesus' name. As the Scripture says that weeping may endure for a night but joy comes in the morning, I pray that the Lord will perform the work of physical, emotional, psychological, mental, marital and financial healing, restoration and regeneration upon your life this very night, in the name of Jesus.

2. Growth of mankind

Has it ever occurred to you how or when people grow in height or weight? Or let me put it better, have you ever seen anybody suddenly growing or shrinking before your very eyes in the day? I doubt you have. Yet people grow; otherwise, we all would have remained babies forever. The reason you have not seen anyone growing an inch taller naturally before your very eyes is that it is the nighttime that God has reserved for this marvelous work in our lives. It is one of the powers and wonders of nighttime that I want you to pay particular attention to.

It is a deep truth, which even science validates, that growth hormones in humans are secreted at very high levels at night when we are deeply asleep. In one interesting study, a group of researchers studied the secretion of growth hormones in humans during the day and compared it to what happened at night, and they found that there is a remarkable spike in the release of the growth hormones at night. Similarly, in a recent study featured on the BBC, researchers found that "growth plates" in children and adolescents become at ease during night sleep, paving the way for their elongation and consequently, growth of the children and young adults.

As if to confirm this, Dr. Jeremy Wales, a consultant pediatrician, who has studied child growth at Sheffield Children's Hospital, said: "There have been human studies that also document this. Children do have growth spurts at night." Simply put, the power for growth has been embedded by God into the night hours.

So, then you know that the demonic forces do not have complete control over the night. Despite their activities, you can tap into their power for growth and advance every area of your life. I pray for you that you will experience such supernatural and miraculous growth "in wisdom and stature, and in favor with God and men" in Jesus' name. (Luke 2:52). Since nighttime is designed for growth, your life will experience all-around growth, regardless of the activities of the demonic kingdom, in the name of Jesus.

3. Fruitfulness of vegetation

How and when do plants grow and produce fruits for human consumption and sustenance? Jesus gives us a clue of this in Mark 4:26-29, "And He said, "The kingdom of God is as if a man should scatter seed on the ground, and should sleep by night and rise by day, and the seed should sprout and grow, he himself does not know how. For the earth yields crops by itself: first the blade, then the head, after that the full grain in the head. But when the grain ripens, immediately he puts in the sickle, because the harvest has come."

Wow, what an awesome God we serve! Even though the ultimate thrust of the above parable is the wondrous growth and advancement of God's Kingdom, we can glean a lot from the literal illustration. Indeed, Christ intended to show us that it is the same mysterious or miraculous way in which plants seem to grow from mere seeds to flourishing vegetation that the Kingdom of God blossoms.

So, what makes the process of plant growth and fruitfulness not only miraculous but also mysterious to us? It is because the process happens mostly during the night hours. This was what the Lord meant when He said, "and should sleep by night and rise by day, and the seed should sprout and grow". Observe that the process of sprouting and growing happens between the time of sleeping at night and rising by day. In confirmation of this, when asked how and when plants, grow, an expert said, "The absence of light actually stimulates plants to grow fastest at night. Plant phytochromes detect darkness, encouraging growth hormone production, and causing the plant to elongate in search of light. The same process helps plants orientate their foliage to light and helps seedlings stretch in search of light."

This reveals that the night hours are imbued with the capacity for abundant flourishing, fruitfulness, breaking out and bursting forth, and that capacity has not and cannot in any way be altered by the satanic kingdom. This is another compelling proof of the sovereignty of God, which should not only give you assurance but encourage you to tap into this awesome power to cause a mighty breakthrough in all areas of your life. You can experience uncommon and unprecedented breakthrough in all areas of your life where there have been limitations and brick walls, if you can latch on to this power of the night!

4. **Divine revelations, communication and impartation**

Deuteronomy 29:29 says, "The secret things belong to the Lord our God, but those things which are revealed belong to us and to our children forever…" There are so many secret things about our lives, families, ministries, communities and nations that the Lord, out of His mercies, wants to bring to our knowledge. These secrets are usually to protect, assure, forewarn, guide or bring mighty deliverances to us. One of the common ways in which the Lord communicates such "secret things" is through dreams at night. Moreover, in certain instances, this communication from God comes with life-changing impartations, as well as destiny discovery or recovery.

Let me quickly say that there is a reason we are considering this divine revelation of the night under the mercies of God, and not under the special interventions of God, which will be our focus in the next chapter. The reason is that such revelations are a universal occurrence, as God not only brings them to His children but, for particular reasons, even to those who haven't known Him. Job 33:15-16 says, "In a dream, in a vision of the night, When deep sleep falls upon men, While slumbering on their beds, Then He opens the ears of men, And seals their instruction."

The Bible contains several instances of this demonstration of God's mercy and sovereignty. Indeed, about 21 mentions of God communicating with people through dreams are recorded in the Scripture. What is most interesting, however, is that virtually all of these instances happened in the night, bringing us to the understanding again that the night still belongs to our unchanging God.

In Genesis 20, God appeared to Melchizedek to let him know that he and his household were in trouble for keeping Sarah, Abraham's wife with him, albeit unknowingly. In Genesis 28, while Jacob was going to be with Laban, in Padan Aram, God appeared to him in a dream of the night to assure him of His presence and the blessings that would come upon him and his descendants. In Genesis 31, God appeared again to

Jacob and told him it was time to leave Laban. In that same chapter, God appeared to Laban in a dream of the night and warned him never to harass Jacob who he had been pursuing.

We also know of the popular and powerful dreams of Joseph, in which God communicated his destiny to him (Genesis 37). Of course, we are not told of the exact time of the day in which he had the dream; but shortly after, we are told, in Genesis 40, that Pharaoh's former baker and former cupbearer, both of who had been imprisoned alongside Joseph, had very significant dreams in the night. As with all the previous cases, we have seen, the dreams were to communicate to them important messages about their lives – which eventually came to manifestation, as Joseph had predicted.

Very interestingly, Pharaoh himself became the next recipient of this special nightly revelation from God, to be recorded in the Scripture. In Genesis 41, God showed him two different but related dreams. As we eventually discover, the dreams were meant to forewarn the world, and the land of Egypt, in particular, of impending years of excruciating famine, after the first few years of abundant harvest. Unsurprisingly, the revelation did not come to him during the day but in the dead of night. As the Bible reveals, "…So Pharaoh awoke, and indeed, it was a dream. Now it came to pass in the morning that his spirit was troubled, and he sent and called for all the magicians of Egypt and all its wise men…" (Genesis 41:7-8).

There are many more of such revelations and impartations by night in the Bible, including the great encounter that turned the life of Solomon into a record-breaking wonder (1 Kings 3:5-15). And the list goes on.

One thing that should have registered on your mind by now is that these incidents, mostly happening at night, couldn't have been coincidences. Rather, they are further proof of the fact that the nighttime is truly not an ordinary time. God designed it from the beginning to be a time when many blessings of the day are molded and set in motion. Indeed, we can say that just as the spiritual controls the physical, it is the night that controls the day. Destinies are birthed and quenched in the hours of the night. Sicknesses are implanted and uprooted in the night. The seeds of progress and retrogression are all implanted in the night. This is why you must never joke about these hours. More so, as we will see in later chapters, you must avoid the mistakes and abuse of the night – so as to avoid its dangers, while cooperating with God in all earnest so as to reap the many befits embedded in it.

But we are not done yet. Let's consider more of the mercies of the night bestowed on us by the majesty of God's sovereignty.

5. Ideas and inspirations

This is one of the most remarkable mercies that God freely bestows on humanity at night. Something I want you to note from the emphasis I have been making about the universality of the divine mercies of the night is that, if God could decide to make these mercies available to even those who do not know Him, then you who are His legitimate child (if you have been born again) should enjoy them so much more and this is why you must not leave things to chance. You must ask. You must seek and you must knock. "For everyone who asks receives, and he who seeks finds, and to him who knocks it will be opened" (Matthew 7:8).

Now to the ideas and inspirations of the night. Did you know that many of the great breakthroughs of science, inventions of technology, as well as the masterpieces of the arts, music and literature actually came from inspirations and ideas received in the hours of the night? Take Google, for example. As Larry Page, who initially conceived the idea, once revealed, the inspiration for the revolutionary search engine came to him right in the middle of the night! Here are his exact words:

 "You know what it's like to wake up in the middle of the night with a vivid dream? And you know how, if you don't have a pencil and pad by the bed to write it down, it will be completely gone the next morning? Well, I had one of those dreams when I was 23. When I suddenly woke up, I was thinking: what if we could download the whole web, and just keep the links; and I grabbed a pen and started writing! Sometimes it is important to wake up and stop dreaming. I spent the middle of that night scribbling out the details and convincing myself it would work…Amazingly, I had no thought of building a search engine. The idea wasn't even on the radar. But, much later we now have a better way of ranking webpages to make a really great search engine, and Google was born. When a really great dream shows up, grab it!"

Wow, the mercies of the night. I pray for you that, by God's sovereign benevolence and omnipotence the night will bring you world-changing ideas and destiny-changing inspirations, in the name of Jesus.

What happened to Larry was similar to what happened to the renowned Russian chemist, Dmitri Mendeleev, who formulated the periodic table of element that has become the cornerstone of the field of Chemistry. According to him, it was on one night that he saw all the elements that he had battled to arrange for long into place on a table. He produced a draft of what he saw and the understanding of Chemistry and the atomic structure has never been the same again.

Moreover, some of the contents of John Bunyan's immortal classic, *Pilgrim's Progress* were influenced by the inspiration of the night. So also was Albert Einstein's popular Theory of Relativity and other discoveries that have changed our world. What all this confirms is that the night is suffused with an avalanche of ideas and inspirations from heaven that are seeking where they can be incubated and birthed into the world. I pray that you will be the next in line to get ideas that will transform your life, business, family, ministry, finances and community, in the name of Jesus.

6. Solutions to complex problems

One of the greatest Christian scientists of all time, George Washington Carver, once said, *"I would often go to sleep with an apparently insoluble problem. When I woke the answer was there."* I don't know how often this has happened to you too. But I can confirm that it is true. Many times we go to bed at night, thinking our world is going to crash because of an experience or dilemma that seems unsolvable or unbearable. But then, lo and behold, the morning comes and it seems as if the scales have suddenly gone off our eyes and our mental faculties have been rejigged.

If you have been wondering what causes this, then you have the answer right here. The night is imbued with the power of God to ease our burdens and bring incredible solutions to the issues that agitate us. According to psychologists from the University of California in San Diego, night sleep improves our ability to come up with creative solutions to problems by assisting the brain in flagging unrelated ideas and memories and forging connections among them.

But while scientists believe that these nightly solutions can only come from sleep, I can assure you that you can easily activate them when you take hold of the night with the power of God and cause its power for breakthrough to be released upon you. You can bend the night in your favor if you will join the mighty men and women who have enjoyed and are still enjoying the manifold blessings that God unleashes upon mankind within those dark hours when many are cut off from their place.

Prayer Points

1. I worship you Lord because you are the merciful and sovereign God, who rules and reigns over the universe.
2. Thank you Lord because your works and purposes for mankind in the day and at night remain unchanged, despite the activities of the demonic kingdom.
3. I declare that the abundance of the mercies of the night, as well as of the day, are mine in the name of Jesus.
4. I declare divine healing, rejuvenation and restoration of the night upon my spirit, soul, body and mind, in the name of Jesus.
5. I receive supernatural anointing for growth and flourishing, inspiration and solution in all areas of my life, in the name of Jesus.

Chapter 4

MIRACLES FOR THE REDEEMED

"But thus saith the Lord, Even the captives of the mighty shall be taken away, and the prey of the terrible shall be delivered: for I will contend with him that contendeth with thee, and I will save thy children."

(Psalms 91:10-11, KJV)

We must now step up higher from the general mercies of the night to the marvelous miracles, victories and breakthroughs that God specifically performs in the lives and circumstances of His children within these hours. In doing so, we move from the natural to the supernatural, from the ordinary to the extraordinary.

Since nighttime has become a significant time in which the demonic powers strategize and execute their destructive agendas upon mankind, it has invariably become the time when the Almighty God, whose love for His children is unrivalled and unfailing, carries out some of the greatest miracles of intervention and deliverances in their lives. The Bible is replete with proofs of these mighty interventions, and we will be examining some of them here. As a child of the Living God, you must begin to see the manifold possibilities and privileges that you can take advantage of.

Let each of the following spectacular moves of the omnipotent God rouse your faith and convince you that there are no impossible battles, situations, dilemmas, oppositions, challenges, barricades or confrontations with the Almighty God. Indeed, as you behold these wonders of the Most High in the lives of His children with a heart of faith, the Jericho walls of your life will begin to crumble and all the Goliaths and strong men that contend with your life and destiny will bow to the authority of the Lord of Hosts, in the name of Jesus.

Divine Interventions of the Night

1. Life-changing visitations

It is quite remarkable that when Jacob wanted to give an account of the journey of his life to Joseph in Genesis 48, he did not begin with all that had happened to him in his younger years. Rather, he started from what happened the night that God first visited him in Genesis 28. Do you know why? Because that was the time his life REALLY began.

Jacob knew it himself that, until that night, his life had been without meaning, purpose or direction. But on that particular night, his life experienced an unforgettable turnaround and everything began to fall in place. That was why he declared, as the end of his life on earth drew near: "God Almighty appeared to me at Luz in the land of Canaan and blessed me…" (Genesis 48:3). I pray for you that you too will experience this destiny-changing visitation from God, such that the testimony of your life will begin to revolve around it.

Indeed, visitations of the night are a common way God that causes mighty breakthroughs in the life of His children. It would interest you to know that another unforgettable milestone in the life of Jacob also happened on another night that God visited him at Jabbok. That was the night of the mighty combat and revelation that that changed his destiny and got him a new name (Genesis 32:22-31). It was that night that marked the climax of all the blessings that had begun to pour into his life from the time he first encountered God in the night. It was that night that the Israel that had been trapped in him was finally unchained, and his place among the company of the blessed was permanently sealed.

I don't know how long you have been living in emptiness, not knowing what your real purpose is or what direction your life should be taking. I guarantee you that a single all-night encounter with God can cause the change of a lifetime in your life because there is power in the night. I pray for you that, like Jacob, you will receive such amazing visitation from God in the hours of the night that will mark a turning point of you, bring clarity to your life and unleash your destiny.

2. Affliction of your Troublers

"For thus says the LORD of hosts: "He sent Me after glory, to the nations which plunder you; for he who touches you touches the apple of His eye. For surely I will shake My hand against them, and they shall become spoil for their servants..." (Zechariah 2:8-9). The Lord of Hosts never toys with any of His precious children. And knowing how strategic the night is in the spirit realm, He moves mightily at this time around the camps of the wicked ones to not only confound their devices against us, but to also fight for us and inflict untold affliction, devastation amd lamentations in their midst.

The Scripture contains proofs of this special nightly intervention of God for our sake. Consider the case of the Israelites who had been oppressed, tormented and confined by the Egyptians for so many years. Every attempt to get Pharaoh to release these people of God had little or no effect on him – until the night that God rose in His majesty and smote the Egyptians so fearfully that the entire nation was plunged into prolonged anguished and lamentation.

Here is how it happened: "And it came to pass at midnight that the LORD struck all the firstborn in the land of Egypt, from the firstborn of Pharaoh who sat on his throne to the firstborn of the captive who was in the dungeon, and all the firstborn of livestock. So Pharaoh rose in the night, he, all his servants, and all the Egyptians; and there was a great cry in Egypt, for there was not a house where there was not one dead…

And the Egyptians urged the people, that they might send them out of the land in haste. For they said, "We shall all be dead." (Exodus 12:29-33).

What an awesome God we serve! The enemies had no choice but to let go of God's people because God struck them at a time and in a way they had not expected. And to prove to you that what happened above wasn't an isolated case but a demonstration of what God regularly does for His children, let me show you another powerful example from the Scripture. This time around, it was Sennacherib and the Assyrians who were plotting to invade and terrorize the people of God. But as God's people called upon Him in all earnestness, He was moved with compassion and gave this assurance: ""Therefore thus says the LORD concerning the king of Assyria: 'He shall not come into this city, Nor shoot an arrow there, Nor come before it with shield, Nor build a siege mound against it. By the way that he came, By the same shall he return; And he shall not come into this city,' Says the LORD. 'For I will defend this city, to save it For My own sake and for My servant David's sake.' " (2 Kings 19:32-34).

Of course, as you can trust, God certainly made good His promise, and He chose the midnight hour to do it again. "And it came to pass on a certain night that the angel of the LORD went out, and killed in the camp of the Assyrians one hundred and eighty-five thousand; and when people arose early in the morning, there were the corpses—all dead. So Sennacherib king of Assyria departed and went away, returned home, and remained at Nineveh. Now it came to pass, as he was worshiping in the temple of Nisroch his god, that his sons Adrammelech and Sharezer struck him down with the sword; and they escaped into the land of Ararat. Then Esarhaddon his son reigned in his place" (2 Kings 19:35-37).

This is the same way the Lord will visit the camps of your oppressors and tormentors and unleash the terror of His fury upon them until they cease to be a thorn in your flesh. He has declared, "I will feed those who oppress you with their own flesh, And they shall be drunk with their own blood as with sweet wine. All flesh shall know That I, the LORD, am your Savior, And your Redeemer, the Mighty One of Jacob." (Isaiah 49:26). And so shall it be, in the mighty name of Jesus.

3. Breaking of chains, yokes and prison doors

The Lord who cannot lie has declared in Isaiah 10:27, "And it shall come to pass in that day, that his burden shall be taken away from off thy shoulder, and his yoke from off thy neck, and the yoke shall be destroyed because of the anointing." There is sufficient evidence to prove that He does this best in the midnight hour, when He takes the battle right to the camp of the enemies.

Acts 16:25 gives us a graphic picture of the way the mountain-moving, yoke-breaking and chain-melting power of God works for us in the midnight hour: "But at midnight Paul and Silas were praying and singing hymns to God, and the prisoners were listening to them. Suddenly there was a great earthquake, so that the foundations of the prison were shaken; and immediately all the doors were opened and everyone's chains were loosed." (Acts 16:25-26).

Hallelujah! I declare that you are the next in line for such a move of God as this. May the earthquake from God descend on every prison and barricade of your life. May the foundations of the covens, curses and covenants that limit your progress be dismantled. May every door that has been locked against your glory and promotion be unlocked. And may every chain of addiction, affliction, oppression, limitation and deprivation be loosed from your life, in the name of Jesus!

4. Connection to destiny-helpers and due promotion

This is another amazing way in which God intervenes on behalf of His children in the midnight hour. I mentioned it to you earlier that the activities of the night drive the results we often see during the day. And we have seen equally seen that most of the calamities and devastations that befall mankind are often concocted and concluded within the night hour.

However, it is heartwarming to know that it is not only evil works that are conceived and incubated within this period. Many miracles and breakthroughs of the Almighty God are also set in motion for His children within this time. One of such is the miracle of promotion and connection with those that have been put in place by God to serve as a ladder to our expected destinations.

Here is how it works: "That night the king could not sleep. So one was commanded to bring the book of the records of the chronicles; and they were read before the king. And it was found written that Mordecai had told of Bigthana and Teresh, two of the king's eunuchs, the doorkeepers who had sought to lay hands on King Ahasuerus. Then the king said, "What honor or dignity has been bestowed on Mordecai for this?" And the king's servants who attended him said, "Nothing has been done for him." So the king said, "Who is in the court?" Now Haman had just entered the outer court of the king's palace to suggest that the king hang Mordecai on the gallows that he had prepared for him. The king's servants said to him, "Haman is there, standing in the court." And the king said, "Let him come in." So Haman came in, and the king asked him, "What shall be done for the man whom the king delights to honor?" Now Haman thought in his heart, "Whom would the king delight to honor more than me?" And Haman answered the king, "For the man whom the king delights to honor, let a royal robe be brought which the king has worn, and a horse on which the king has ridden, which has a royal crest placed on its head. Then let this robe and horse be delivered to the hand of one of the king's most noble princes, that he may array the man whom the king delights to honor. Then parade him on horseback through the city square, and proclaim before him: 'Thus shall it be done to the man whom the king delights to honor!' " Then the king said to Haman, "Hurry, take the robe and the horse, as you have suggested, and do so for Mordecai the Jew who sits within the king's gate! Leave nothing undone of all that you have spoken" (Esther 6:1-10).

Here is one thing you must know about warfare from this passage. The battles of life differ from one person to another. While some people are afflicted with failure and underachievement, others – like Mordecai here – have to battle with under-recognition and under-appreciation. This is a serious dimension of demonic bondage that some people do not pay much attention to because of ignorance and lack of discernment.

Can you imagine someone who had done such a great service to the king being forgotten – just like that? Someone who had saved the king from being assassinated! It is very much possible that the king had assumed that his right-hand man, Haman, would have done the needful, not knowing that the same Haman was the greatest contender for the wellbeing of Mordecai. And so, Mordecai remained unknown at the palace gate (edge of breakthrough) when he should have become the most honored man in the kingdom!

There are times people labor so hard, and get so little in return. There are times we are due for promotion, and nothing seems to be forthcoming. There are times we render outstandingly helpful service and we are hardly recognized, much less adequately rewarded. Unfortunately, many of us take these things to be ordinary. Let me tell you, dear friend, most times such abnormalities are not ordinary. There are evil forces, who sometimes use human agents, to frustrate the efforts of talented and hardworking people – such that nobody hears about them or deems it necessary to assist or finance them to greater heights.

But, glory to God, who fights for His children and clears out the barriers of opposition, under-recognition, under-appreciation and forgetfulness that the demonic kingdom uses to hinder their progress and promotion. "That night the king could not sleep" – because the rousing power of God was at work upon his life. I pray for you that from this night, the Lord of Hosts will begin to rouse all your potential helpers from their slumbers. I pray that every Haman opposing your recognition and elevation will be disgraced and confounded, in Jesus' name.

You can also see this connection with destiny helpers from the perspective of being linked to your life-partner. Sometimes, all it takes to find or attract that man or woman that God has purposed for you is just a night of divine intervention. This was what happened between Boaz and Ruth. Ruth 3:7-11 says, "And after Boaz had eaten and drunk, and his heart was cheerful, he went to lie down at the end of the heap of grain; and she came softly, uncovered his feet, and lay down. Now it happened at midnight that the man was startled, and turned himself; and there, a woman was lying at his feet. And he said, "Who are you?" So she answered, "I am Ruth, your maidservant. Take your maidservant under your wing, for you are a close relative." Then he said, "Blessed are you of the LORD, my daughter! For you have shown more kindness at the end than at the beginning, in that you did not go after young men, whether poor or rich. And now, my daughter, do not fear. I will do for you all that you request, for all the people of my town know that you are a virtuous woman."

I tell you, dear reader. Things happen at the midnight, much more than you can imagine. Take advantage of these hours of wonders and be connected to unlimited divine FAVOR and connection, in the name of Jesus.

5. **Power for uncommon exploits**

The midnight hour is a time that many champions are born in the spirit realm. It is the time that those who will do extraordinary exploits within the day connect to the very Source of power and download the strength of heaven into their very being. Isaiah 40:28-31 says, "Have you not known? Have you not heard? The everlasting God, the LORD, The Creator of the ends of the earth, Neither faints nor is weary. His understanding is unsearchable. He gives power to the weak, And to those who have no might He increases strength. Even the youths shall faint and be weary, And the young men shall utterly fall, But those who wait on the LORD Shall renew their strength; They shall mount up with wings like eagles, They shall run and not be weary, They shall walk and not faint."

There are different levels of tasks, challenges and burdens we have to deal with from day to day, as human beings. Each of these requires different levels of ability to successfully handle and overcome. However, when it is time to execute uncommon exploits that go beyond the daily routines, the hours of the night have proven to be the defining moment when God equips, empowers and fortifies us against failure and breakdown. Look at the life of our Lord Jesus Christ, as an example. His was an uncommon mission, with many temptations and oppositions but He maintained a consistent level of power and dominion throughout His mission because He was a man who understood the power of the prayer of the night.

As the storm of opposition began to gather against Him at the beginning of His ministry and He needed companions to assist in His ministry, He had to spend all night praying for grace, strength and guidance to succeed in the task ahead. And He indeed received daily renewal of strength from heaven to succeed. Again, as His time drew near to go to the cross, we were told that He had to go to the mountain and spent the night praying. He again received a supernatural recharge of strength, as He was transfigured and Moses and Elijah appeared to Him. And finally on the very night He was to be betrayed, He spent the night praying and the Scripture reveals that "an angel appeared to Him from heaven, strengthening Him" (Luke 22:43).

That supernatural strength from heaven facilitated the triumphant bearing of the shame, agony and heavy burden that came with the cross.

From all the instances we have seen so far, we have full

conviction and assurance that the night hours can be to our maximum favor and blessing, if only we cooperate with God to get the best from it. To do this, we need to consider a few important truths in the next chapter.

Prayer Points

1. I give glory to you, Lord, for your mighty intervention on behalf of your children in the night hours.

2. I declare that, from tonight, my life will be open to uncommon visitations from the Throne of Grace.

3. I decree divine afflictions, terrors and firestorms upon every demonic individual, groups and covens that are after my life, family, finances and ministry, in the name of Jesus.

4. I pronounce a total collapse of every yoke, mountain, barrier and shackle that has held me bound, in the name of Jesus.

5. I connect to my destiny-helpers by the power of the Most High God, in the name of Jesus.

Chapter 5

MISTAKES COMMON TO THE NIGHT HOURS

"Lest Satan should take advantage of us; for we are not ignorant of his devices."

(2 Corinthians 2:11)

Now that we know of the abundant possibilities and miracles that we can enjoy within the hours of the night, we should want to know how to be regular partakers of these heavenly interventions. We will be looking at this in a short while, but first we must consider some wrong notions and wrong ways of using our night. This will help us in two ways. One, it will help us not to continue to be victims of the enemy's nightly manipulation. Two, it will help us to know what we should be doing with our night. It goes without saying that once we are aware of the wrong ways of perceiving and managing our nights, then we automatically have an idea of what we should be doing right.

Let me re-emphasize that the reason the demonic kingdom easily takes advantage of some people at night is because of ignorance and laziness. These loopholes manifest in the following ways:

1. Excessive sleep

Some people erroneously believe that nighttime is still a time to sleep for several hours at a go. Some even take sleeping pills to enjoy extended sleep. What such people do not realize is that they are exposing themselves, their destinies and their loved ones to an unhindered flow of demonic manipulations.

Well, don't be surprised by what I've just stated. It is not an invented or assumed notion; it is a truth that is deeply rooted in the Scripture. In fact, what you would find even more interesting is that even God who created sleep warns against excess of it. Now, this is something you should take very seriously because, as I have earlier revealed, it has been the cause of repeated defeat and prolonged affliction in the lives of many.

You see, ordinarily, manufacturers do not like to say something negative about their own product, for fear of a backlash or decreased patronage. This is why, when a manufacturer is sincere enough to reveal the negative side of his own product, then it is something you must be gravely concerned about.

Make no mistake about it – because many people are doing so and paying dearly for it – God, the manufacturer of sleep, says if you love sleep, you will come to poverty. "Do not love sleep, lest you come to poverty; Open your eyes, and you will be satisfied with bread" (Proverbs 20:13). The Scripture minces no word on this. The sleeping state has become a battlefield, and an easy avenue for poverty and misery to creep upon an individual. This is not just in the physical but also in the spiritual. Note that poverty here has layers of meaning. And you can summarize it to include all the evils that come upon man-like prowlers while in the sleeping state. This is why the Scripture warns against excess of sleep. "But while men slept, his enemy came and sowed tares among the wheat and went his way" (Matthew 13:25).

Let's return to the story of the two harlots in 1 Kings 3 again, so you can get a better picture of the damage that sleep is doing to many lives and families. We were told that one of the women slept so much that she didn't know when she was killing her own child. I can tell you clearly that many have slept and continue to sleep on their own glory and destiny. Many who should have become great men and women have missed it because they thought they knew sleep better than the One who created it. Great opportunities have passed them by because they cannot do without extended night sleep. The pregnancy of greatness of many that should have been birthed has either been aborted by the forces of darkness or ended in stillbirth because they cannot sacrifice a few hours of night sleep on warfare or other necessary meaningful activities.

Some have slept on the great visions, ideas and inspirations that God gave to them in the hours of the night, rather than acting on them. Consider the case of the Google founder that I told you about earlier on. Remember those words of his, "You know what it's like to wake up in the middle of the night with a vivid dream? And you know how, if you don't have a pencil and pad by the bed to write it down, it will be completely gone the next morning?" Many get such dreams, but because of excessive sleep, the enemy steals it away from them before they wake up from their prolonged sleep – and thus they continue to languish in poverty and stagnancy. I pray this will not be your portion.

In worse scenarios, some have slept on and killed their children and spouses spiritually because they could not spare a few hours of the night to intercede and agonize on their behalf. And also, as the examples of Samson and King Saul (Judges 16:9; 1 Samuel 26:1-12) show, some have slept and never knew when their sources of success, strength, power, influence, defense and progress have been stolen from them – leaving them empty and helpless.

2. Ignoring negative dreams and visions

I mentioned earlier that nighttime is a time of communication and revelations. Many times God allows us to clearly see the sorry state of our lives or warns us of some impending calamities being planned against us in the kingdom of darkness. Sadly however many just dismiss these nightly revelations or just mumble some wishy-washy prayers about them. This is a very costly mistake of the night, which many have paid dearly for.

Consider the case of Eli in 1 Samuel 3:10-18: "Now the LORD came and stood and called as at other times, "Samuel! Samuel!" And Samuel answered, "Speak, for Your servant hears." Then the LORD said to Samuel: "Behold, I will do something in Israel at which both ears of everyone who hears it will tingle. In that day I will perform against Eli all that I have spoken concerning his house, from beginning to end. For I have told him that I will judge his house forever for the iniquity which he knows, because his sons made themselves vile, and he did not restrain them. And therefore I have sworn to the house of Eli that the iniquity of Eli's house shall not be atoned for by sacrifice or offering forever." So Samuel lay down until morning, and opened the doors of the house of the LORD. And Samuel was afraid to tell Eli the vision. Then Eli called Samuel and said, "Samuel, my son!" He answered, "Here I am." And he said, "What is the word that the LORD spoke to you? Please do not hide it from me. God do so to you, and more also, if you hide anything from me of all the things that He said to you." Then Samuel told him everything, and hid nothing from him. And he said, "It is the LORD. Let Him do what seems good to Him."

Sadly, Eli allowed all these foreseen catastrophes to consume him and his household. This is the same nonchalant attitude that some people manifest when they have some disturbing visions and nightmares.

They simply heave a sigh of relief that "it was just a dream" or simply ask that the will of God be done. This is a dangerous attitude. The evil you do not confront will definitely confront you, sooner or later.

Don't shrug off warnings of the night. Dreams that involve serpents, swimming, picking snails or plucking chili, having sexual intercourse, picking money on the ground, being naked or being chased by wild beasts or evil creatures and similar dreams are not such that can be toyed with. They signify present battles or coming calamities and must be immediately and violently countered by the power of the Almighty God.

3. Ignoring the Spirit's prompting to pray

There are times when the Lord, out of His unfailing mercies, alerts us in the night to pray, especially to nullify some evil counsel being orchestrated against us at that time. Sometimes, it comes as a sudden jolt from sleep or at other times as a gentle nudge. It just happens that sleep is temporarily halted from our eyes and the Holy Spirit begins to quicken our spirit to begin to pray either for ourselves or on behalf of someone else.

Unfortunately, rather than take advantage of this gracious mercy of the Holy Spirit, many simply choose to cause sleep to return to them, until it finally comes and the evil ones complete the project they were planning over their lives. This is what leads to demonic invasion, breakdowns and sudden devastations in many lives and homes. And the cause is often spiritual laziness and lack of discernment. "I went by the field of the lazy man, And by the vineyard of the man devoid of understanding; And there it was, all overgrown with thorns; Its surface was covered with nettles; Its stone wall was broken down. When I saw it, I considered it well; I looked on it and received instruction: A little sleep, a little slumber, A little folding of the hands to rest; So shall your poverty come like a prowler, and your need like an armed man" (Proverbs 24:30-34).

I pray that you too receive instruction, dear reader. So that the field of your life, home and ministry will not be overtaken by thorns or invaded by the satanic kingdom.

4. Believing the lies of science

This is a very deadly mistake that has continued to ruin individuals, families and even nations. Truth be told, the awesome place of science in our world cannot be denied. The theories, principles and discoveries of science and technology have made life easier and better and have helped to explain many events of life that would otherwise have seemed mysterious and confusing to us.

But science can be destructive in certain instances. And the most common of these is when science, which has been given by God to explain natural phenomena, wants to displace its creator by attempting to deny or dabble into the realm of the supernatural. Let me break this down for you. Science is meant to explain the natural and physical world – that is, the visible world and you can rely on it to that extent. But when science tries to explain, as it sometimes tries to, spiritual or supernatural occurrences, then steer clear of it because if you follow its explanations, you may open the door to irreparable damage in your life and destiny.

Why am I saying this? I heard and read some very laughable but destructive attempts by scientists to explain some spiritual issues. Take the issue of demonic oppression at night for instance, which some "experts" have simply tried to explain away as "sleep paralysis". Here is one such destructive explanation: "Sleep paralysis is a condition in which a person is mentally conscious but physically unable to move. It is sometimes accompanied by hallucinations of frightening invaders in the bedroom. The result is a scary, almost nightmarish experience of sensing an intruder but being unable to respond. Thankfully, this is nothing more than the product of a half-awake brain." Another explanation goes: "Sleep paralysis occurs when a person is just falling asleep or waking up. During these transitions, you may find that you are unable to move or speak for a few seconds or as long as several minutes. Some people sweat, or even have a sense of choking and being unable to breathe."

Did you see that? Despite all the factors that point to the contrary, scientists want you to believe that an occurrence, as physically and psychologically disturbing as this, is a "normal" experience. The same goes for sexual encounters in dreams. Many scientists and psychologists would say these are "perfectly normal and even healthy". When recently, a doctor claimed that demons could have intercourse with humans, many of her colleagues and others in the media considered her to be deranged. These are lies of science, and if you believe them, it will be at your peril. This is why someone says that "demons prefer anonymity. They would rather that you would characterize that behavior as a psychological disorder. They really don't want you to know they're there. They don't want to be exposed."

As I stated above, this tendency of believing the lies of science has been the ruin of many destinies and families. Sometimes children exhibit abnormal behaviors that could only have come from demonic deposits in their systems or outright possession, but parents simply rush them to see doctors and psychologists, who, most times, mislead them into believing that the children are normal and are just "trying to express themselves" or they may give them the impression that medicine can cure them. Unfortunately, by the time the parents realize the futility of such claims, irreparable damage has been done. We must be wise and discerning. Not every occurrence has a scientific explanation or a medical solution. Spiritual maladies can only be cured by spiritual remedies!

5. Sleeping at prayer vigils

This is another mistake of the night that some people make. There are times when warfare prayer vigils are organized and while the atmosphere is charged with the power of God, with demons being cast out and all manners of curses and demonic deposits being uprooted, some people just spend their time sleeping.

This can prove very dangerous, and the sleeper could end up going back home worse that he or she was before attending the vigil.

Look at this case, for example: "Now on the first day of the week, when the disciples came together to break bread, Paul, ready to depart the next day, spoke to them and continued his message until midnight. There were many lamps in the upper room where they were gathered together. And in a window sat a certain young man named Eutychus, who was sinking into a deep sleep. He was overcome by sleep; and as Paul continued speaking, he fell down from the third story and was taken up dead. But Paul went down, fell on him, and embracing him said, "Do not trouble yourselves, for his life is in him." (Acts 20:7-10).

Of course, while this wasn't really a prayer vigil and while the incident could be considered mere physical accident, the fact remains that many "spiritual accidents" also occur this way, when people sleep where they should not at the midnight hour. Prayer vigils are battlegrounds, not sleeping grounds!

I pray you will not receive spiritual injury where you should be receiving elevation, in the name of Jesus.

6. Watching horror, violent or erotic shows

Ordinarily, these are not activities that any true believer should be engaging in at any time of the day. But the nighttime poses much more dangers than many people think and if you consider such shows as mere entertainment, you may be setting yourself up for demonic visitation or even possession. Your eyes and ears are windows to your subconscious; and feeding your subconscious (or spirit man) with poison, could end up poisoning your entire life.

Interestingly, even scientific and psychological proofs exist to show that feeding the mind with wrong images, while generally unhealthy, is particularly dangerous at night. For example, in a study recently published in the journal, *Dreaming*, the researchers found that those who viewed violent media before bed were 13 times more likely to have violent dreams that night compared to people who didn't watch violence before bed. They also found that people who had seen sexual content before bed were six times more likely to have sexual dreams.

Now there is an instructive statement made by the leader of that study which carries a very deep meaning that even he was not aware of. According to him, the findings didn't prove violent TV shows, movies or video games cause bad dreams. "People whose dreams tend toward violence may be drawn to those same things in media, or some third factor might explain the connection".

Well, that "third factor" which science cannot explain because of its limitations, is the spiritual angle to these shows. Such images create easy loopholes in people's lives through which the forces of darkness penetrate and inflict their destructions. So, you must be careful not to be the one to invite avoidable battles, crises and demonic invasions into your life and home.

MISTAKES COMMON TO THE NIGHT HOURS

Now that we know the don'ts of the night hour, we can proceed to the principles for making the most of these precious hours of the night!

Prayer Points

1. Thank you, Lord, for opening my eyes to the pitfalls of the night that I must avoid.

2. I receive grace and discernment to escape the snares of the night in the name of Jesus.

3. I ask for forgiveness and cleansing in all the areas I have misused my nights in the past, in the name of Jesus.

4. I renounce all the lies of science and the ignorant that have ensnared me in the past, in the name of Jesus.

5. I desist from every habit, practice and indulgences that have made my nights unprofitable, in the name of Jesus.

Chapter 6

MAKING YOUR NIGHTS VICTORIOUS

"For though we walk in the flesh, we do not war according to the flesh. For the weapons of our warfare are **not** *carnal but mighty in God for pulling down strongholds, casting down arguments and every high thing that exalts itself against the knowledge of God, bringing every thought into captivity to the obedience of Christ."*

(2 Corinthians 10:3-5)

A careful study will reveal to you that most great men and women of power and impact in history and contemporary times are people who understand the power of the night. Such people understand that nighttime is a "goldmine" of resources, treasures and wonders, which fortunately only very few are in contention for. Indeed, the resources of the night are often in excess because not many take advantage of them.

Why do you think communication and broadcast signals are often clearer at night? Why do you think data downloads are usually faster at night? Why do night journeys seem faster? It's all because majority of humanity would have naturally succumbed to the pull of nature and most will prefer to be this way till daybreak. But there are usually a few who dare to defy the weakness of their flesh and the call of nature to take the bull by the horn and do the extraordinary, in order to get extraordinary results.

What activities do these men and women engage in to get the night to yield its best to them? We will examine these, using the Scripture as our guide. However, before then, let's make a quick clarification.

No Contradiction Here

We have earlier emphasized the importance of night rest, as well as the supernatural works that God performs on humans and the whole of nature within the night hours. You may then begin to wonder, should we not rest at night in order to become great in life? Should we go on extended sleepless nights because we want to enjoy uncommon blessings? My answer to that is, not at all.

As we have revealed in the previous chapter, night sleep is good because it is healthful and rejuvenating, aside from numerous other functions. However, there are situations and circumstances that warrant that we temporarily sacrifice our sleeping time to get them resolved. In fact, as we shall soon see, God not only expects that we make this sacrifice but actually commands it. So, while we must sleep as humans, we must understand that there are times when sleep can be costly, if not deadly.

But, then, even aside from sometimes taking advantage of the peculiarities of the night hours to resolve knotty issues, we must also understand that the kind of sleep that most of the great achievers of life give themselves to is that of necessity and not of luxury. In other words, having known that the state of sleep, especially at night, has become a battlefield where poverty, failure and the forces of darkness seek to prevail on man's destiny, then we must sleep, not as the ignorant but as the well informed. This means that even in sleep we cannot afford to completely lose our guard.

Let me show you how this works, with a case study provided by God Himself. Judges 7:1-7 reads: "Then Jerubbaal (that is, Gideon) and all the people who were with him rose early and encamped beside the well of Harod, so that the camp of the Midianites was on the north side of them by the hill of Moreh in the valley. And the LORD said to Gideon, "The people who are with you are too many for Me to give the Midianites into their hands, lest Israel claim glory for itself against Me, saying, 'My own hand has saved me.' Now therefore, proclaim in the hearing of the people, saying, Whoever is fearful and afraid, let him turn and depart at once from Mount Gilead.' " And twenty-two thousand of the people returned, and ten thousand remained. But the LORD said to Gideon, "The people are still too many; bring them down to the water, and I will test them for you there. Then it will be, that of whom I say to you, 'This one shall go with you,' the same shall go with you; and of whomever I say to you, 'This one shall not go with you,' the same shall not go." So he brought the people down to the water. And the LORD said to Gideon, "Everyone who laps from the water with his tongue, as a dog laps, you shall set apart by himself; likewise everyone who gets down on his knees to drink." And the number of those who lapped, putting their hand to their mouth, was three hundred men; but all the rest of the people got down on their knees to drink water. Then the LORD said to Gideon, "By the three hundred men who lapped I will save you, and deliver the Midianites into your hand. Let all the other people go, every man to his place."

It is my prayer for you that, like the 300 men approved by God in the above passage, God will count you worthy to be among the true warriors and champions who will prevail in the battles of the night with His mighty power. But then, you must observe what marked out those 300 men, and understand how God wants you to handle the night sleep He has provided for you. It was God Himself who commanded that the soldiers be taken to the fountain of water to drink. They needed the water to refresh, reinvigorate and prepare them for the battle ahead, just like we need sleep to prepare us for the tasks ahead of us in each new day. Yet, God was observing how they handled the gracious provision He had made. While the majority got lost in the refreshment and relaxation that the drinking provided, the 300 never lost focus of who they were and what they were meant to be doing – hence they remained vigilant even as they drank.

So, there is no contradiction here. The night hours are primarily for your rest and relaxation but the rest and relaxation must be done in knowledge and watchfulness, not in ignorance and slothfulness. To quote Charles Spurgeon, once again, "When thou sleepest, think that thou art resting on the battlefield; when thou walkest, suspect an ambush in every hedge." That is the life of every successful achiever. That is the life of every triumphant follower of Christ!

Powerful Engagements of the Night

What then are the activities we must engage in within our night hours, apart from sleeping?

1. Warfare prayer

Prayer is the greatest activity we can engage in the midnight hour, and so we shall be spending some time to dwell on it. There are two facts about prayers of the night that must be at the back of your mind at all times. The first is that God expects us to engage in these prayers and the second is that God actually COMMANDS us to pray at night.

How do we know that God expects us to engage in warfare prayer at night? One, we have seen in previous chapters that the Scripture contains ample records of children and servants of God – and above all, our Lord Jesus Christ Himself - who engaged in night prayers and received supernatural results. As 2 Timothy 3:16-17 says "All scripture is given by inspiration of God, and is profitable for doctrine, for reproof, for correction, for instruction in righteousness: That the man of God may be perfect, thoroughly furnished unto all good works."

These examples have been documented for us to understand the path to victory, breakthrough and continued dominion in our walk with God. If Jesus Christ, who was the Son of God and, in fact, God in the flesh could consistently engage in night prayers throughout the course of His ministry, can we do less who are His followers, seeing that "no servant is greater than his master, nor is a messenger greater than the one who sent him" (John 13:16)?

If Jacob's destiny did not change until the nights He encountered and engaged God in prayer, can we choose to ignore midnight prayer and expect every one of our battles to be fought and won successfully? If the chains of Paul and Silas were not broken by mere sleeping and weeping but by praying in the midnight hour, can we expect our case to be different?

The examples and the motivations for night prayers have been laid for us to follow, so we don't have to grope in the dark in determining what options we have in conquering the challenges that confront us. We cannot overrule midnight prayers if we expect to have total, all-round victory in our lives!

The second proof that God expects us to engage in midnight warfare prayers is found in the teachings of our Lord Himself. Christ taught twice about prayer and on each instance, He illustrated how we are expected to pray with examples that include midnight prayer. In the first instance, in which He taught the Lord's prayer, He immediately added this illustration to buttress His message, "Which of you shall have a friend, and go to him at midnight and say to him, 'Friend, lend me three loaves; for a friend of mine has come to me on his journey, and I have nothing to set before him'; and he will answer from within and say, 'Do not trouble me; the door is now shut, and my children are with me in bed; I cannot rise and give to you'? I say to you, though he will not rise and give to him because he is his friend, yet because of his persistence he will rise and give him as many as he needs" (Luke 11:5-8).

Isn't this interesting and very instructive? The Lord was teaching us about approaching God in prayer and the immediate example He used was that of man going to knock at the door of his friend at MIDNIGHT! And He further showed that our midnight prayer shouldn't be casual but fervent and focused by saying that that the knocking friend never gave up until his request was granted!

There you have it – midnight prayer isn't just a must but must be taken as a serious, success-oriented engagement!

But Christ wasn't done yet. Again in teaching about prayer in Luke 18, not only did He say that men ought always to pray – both in the day and in the night – and not to faint, but He actually backed His recommendation with a parable and then concluded with this powerful question and assurance: "And shall God not avenge His own elect who cry out day and night to Him, though He bears long with them? I tell you that He will avenge them speedily." (Luke 18:7-8)

Here again, it is obvious. God expects us to pray in the day and in the night, for as long as it takes to obtain our victory and breakthrough.

However, as I mentioned already, beyond mere expectation, God actually obligates us to engage in midnight prayers, not just for ourselves, but for our homes and ministries. Lamentations 2:19 declares, "Arise, cry out in the night, At the beginning of the watches; Pour out your heart like water before the face of the Lord. Lift your hands toward Him for the life of your young children, who faint from hunger at the head of every street."

This, definitely, isn't an expectation but a command. If we want our children, physical and spiritual, liberated from the grips of addiction, oppression and afflictions, we must engage in midnight combats to rescue them from their captors.

Again, Joel 1:13 commands, "Gird yourselves and lament, you priests; Wail, you who minister before the altar; Come, lie all night in sackcloth, You who minister to my God; For the grain offering and the drink offering. Are withheld from the house of your God." What do we do when the heavens seem shut up against our lives, homes and ministries? Do we keep sleeping and snoring while the enemies rejoice and even scale up their attacks

One truth that must have become obvious to you from the fact that God not only expects but obligates us to engage in midnight prayer is that there are certain circumstances, yokes and battles that can never be conquered until you engage the kingdom of darkness in warfare and prevail in the night hours. As I noted earlier, by background, our battles in life vary. A prince born with a silver spoon in his mouth might not necessarily understand the conversation of no money. Why? It is because he has never experienced a situation of no funds before. However, the poverty-stricken man who has struggled all his life will identify with you quickly when you say no funds. Why? He has been there and understands the feeling.

So, you must understand that, in your life, certain circumstances require that you take midnight prayers very seriously. These include:

- Situations where there is more to it than meets the ordinary.
- When your contemporaries have what you should have but obtaining the same has become a struggle.
- When things that come easily for others become unattainable for you.
- When there is a pattern of mysterious misfor-

tunes. For example, I met a man several years ago that used to lose his job at a particular time of the year. So when that time of the year came, he was always expecting it to happen. If such a pattern exists in your life or family, you should engage in the prayer of the night.

- When matters that should come to easy resolution take longer than necessary. Sometimes people find themselves in countless court cases and then it takes longer than necessary to be resolved. There are forces that elongate matters more than necessary.

I must also emphasize that contrary to what some people believe and practice, you do not have to wait till you have an attack or a bad dream at night before you wake up to pray. Midnight prayer can be defensive or offensive, supplicatory or intercessory. And as it commonly said, attack is the best form of defense. It is much better that as you are prompted by the Spirit of God, you scatter the camps and plans of the wicked ones before they have a chance to launch their attacks against you or your loved ones. Prevention is much better than cure!

2. Sacrifice of praise and worship

In Exodus 15:11, Moses declared, "Who is like You, O LORD, among the gods? Who is like You, glorious in holiness, fearful in praises, doing wonders?" God, indeed, is FEARFUL in praises. If you look again at the mighty midnight deliverance from prison chains that came for Paul and Silas in Acts 16, you will realize that praises to God was one of the key factors.

Praise is one of the most powerful weapons of authority and dominion in the midnight hour. Bill Winston rightly says, "Praise is much more than just music; it is a powerful, spiritual warfare tool. God never meant for you to fight your battles alone—Praise will shift the battle from you to God. Praise gives you strength and stops Satan in his tracks."

Praise works wonders because it magnifies God above enemies and circumstances, brings down God's presence and glory, scatters the camps of the powers of darkness and destroys their works and plans. Most beneficiaries of the miracles of the night can attest to the efficacy of the sacrifice of praise to God in the midnight hour. The Psalmist said, "Through each day the Lord pours his unfailing love upon me, and through each night I sing his songs, praying to God who gives me life." (Psalm 42:8, NLT). What a beautiful cycle of life the Psalmist enjoyed! At night, He communes with God in praise and prayers, and during the day, the blessings roll in for him.

Interestingly, sometimes, all we need to silence the threats of evil forces and overturn their attacks, is just to praise God. As Andrew Wommack says, "Praise isn't like the caboose that just follows what happens, but it's more like the engine of a train that makes things happen." And we find a compelling example of how this works in 2 Chronicles 20:21-24, "And when he had consulted with the people, he appointed those who should sing to the LORD, and who should praise the beauty of holiness, as they went out before the army and were saying: "Praise the LORD, For His mercy endures forever." Now when they began to sing and to praise, the LORD set ambushes against the people of Ammon, Moab, and Mount Seir, who had come against Judah; and they were defeated. For the people of Ammon and Moab stood up against the inhabitants of Mount Seir to utterly kill and destroy them. And when they had made an end of the inhabitants of Seir, they helped to destroy one another. So when Judah came to a place overlooking the wilderness, they looked toward the multitude; and there were their dead bodies, fallen on the earth. No one had escaped."

Can you see what awesome power and victory you can command upon your life and situation through praises to God? The confederacy of enemies that rose up against Judah was truly intimidating and seemed unconquerable. But because the people committed themselves to magnifying the greatness of God above the threats of the enemies, they didn't have to even do any fighting; God did the fighting on their behalf and consequently, not a single enemy escaped the sword of the Almighty.

If you too can find the time to praise and worship God in the night – of course, without having to disturb your neighbors – you will be surprised at how seemingly insurmountable mountains of difficulty will melt away before you, as chaff blown away by the wind!

3. **Edifying reading and meditation**

As already pointed out, the time when we sleep has not prevailed over us at night should not be a time to indulge in unwholesome entertainment or other unproductive activities. Instead of this, we can engage ourselves in reading and meditating on materials that can edify, assure and build up our spirit. And it goes without saying that the Bible occupies the number one position here.

It should, in fact, interest you to know that night reading and meditation on God's word is one of the divine requirements for success and prosperity in life. Joshua 1:8 says, "This Book of the Law shall not depart from your mouth, but you shall meditate in it day and night, that you may observe to do according to all that is written in it. For then you will make your way prosperous, and then you will have good success."

Kind David apparently understood the power and victory that come from doing spiritual meditation in the night hours. He testified, "When I remember You on my bed, I meditate on You in the night watches. Because You have been my help, Therefore in the shadow of Your wings I will rejoice. My soul follows close behind You; Your right hand upholds me. But those who seek my life, to destroy it, Shall go into the lower parts of the earth. They shall fall by the sword; They shall be a portion for jackals." (Psalms 63:6-10).

The story of King Ahasuerus, which we read earlier, also reveals the possibilities that come from reading edifying literature and other materials in the night hours. When the king had trouble sleeping, he indulged himself in beneficial reading: "That night the king could not sleep. So one was commanded to bring the book of the records of the chronicles; and they were read before the king. And it was found written that Mordecai had told of Bigthana and Teresh, two of the king's eunuchs, the doorkeepers who had sought to lay hands on King Ahasuerus" (Esther 6:1-2).

There are many uncommon discoveries you can make when you engage in edifying reading in the hours of the night. There are powerful divine revelations, inspirations, and impartations that you can receive when you feed your spirit man with the right information and knowledge in the hours of the night. Let this be your practice from now on!

4. Write down revelations, visions and inspirations

This is one of the most beneficial activities you can undertake in the hours of the night. God told Prophet Habakkuk, "Write the vision and make it plain on tablets, that he may run who reads it" (Habakkuk 2:2). Making a note of the revelations that God gives you at night, will not only help to keep them in your memory but also spur you into action sooner or later.

The Bible itself is a classic testimonial to the power and impact of writing down your visions and inspirations. Billions of lives have been blessed from generation to generation because a few individuals wrote down the revelations and inspirations that they received from God. As we have also earlier noted, many of the greatest books, innovations and accomplishments of our contemporary world came because some people dared to take note of the ideas and visions that came to them in the night hour.

Don't make the mistake of waiting for daybreak to write, or trusting your memory to keep the details. Many people have lost valuable ideas that could have transformed their lives and blessed their world by making such mistakes. As the Chinese ancient proverb rightly says, "The faintest ink is more powerful than the strongest memory."

Prayer Points

1. Thank you, Father, for showing me the various ways I can make the best of my nights and enjoy unlimited blessings from you.

2. I receive the power and fire for the breakthrough prayer of the night into my life, in Jesus' name.

3. I command every matter concerning my life that is taking longer than necessary to expire now in the name of Jesus.

4. I receive the divine empowerment for mountain-moving praise in my night hours, in the name of Jesus.

5. I command every wicked force in my life to hear the ground of my God and flee in the name of Jesus.

Chapter 7

MISSILES OF NIGHT WARRIORS

"Finally, my brethren, be strong in the Lord and in the power of His might. Put on the whole armor of God, that you may be able to stand against the wiles of the devil."

(Ephesians 6:10-11)

The wonderful revelations and impartations that God has showered upon us in the course of exploring this uncommon subject will not be complete, if we do not consider this crucial aspect. We have said a lot about the powers and possibilities of the night. And in the previous chapter, we considered the spiritual activities that we can engage in to make us constantly enjoy the life-changing moves and interventions of God within this special time.

However, it is important to emphasize that these miracles and breakthroughs of the night are not automatic. They only work for the right people under the right circumstances. These "right people" or the champions of the night are those who possess the keys (missiles) for making these spiritual activities work for them.

As we begin to examine these missiles, let me show you a convincing proof from the Scripture that night prayers or vigils do not automatically guarantee breakthroughs without fulfilling the necessary requirements. 2 Samuel 12:16-18 reads: "David, therefore, pleaded with God for the child, and David fasted and went in and lay all night on the ground. So the elders of his house arose *and went* to him, to raise him up from the ground. But he would not, nor did he eat food with them. Then on the seventh day, it came to pass that the child died..."

Here is a good example of an instance where an all-night prayer proved ineffective. Interestingly, David himself had been a partaker of the blessings and miracles of the night on different occasions. What made this particular case different? Simple – at that time, he was not in right standing with God, especially considering the circumstances leading to the birth of the sick child.

So, what are the missiles that add power and potency to our night engagements?

1. Redemption by the blood

The true warriors and champions of the night are those who have been saved from sin and redeemed by the blood of Jesus. This is what gives us power and authority to challenge and conquer the powers of darkness. Revelation 12:11 says, "And they overcame him by the blood of the Lamb and by the word of their testimony."

Moreover, if you look at all the people we considered previously and many more others who attracted the intervention of the Almighty God into their lives and circumstances in the night hours, you will realize that they were people who had a thriving relationship with God. John 1:12 says, "But as many as received Him, to them He gave the right to become children of God (John 1:12). Only children of God have "the authority to trample on serpents and scorpions, and over all the power of the enemy" (Luke 10:19). And you only become a child of God when you sincerely acknowledge your sinfulness, turn to God in sincere repentances, ask for the cleansing of the blood of Jesus and completely forsake sinful living.

Being born into a Christian family, attending church regularly or even being a worker in church does not automatically make you a child of God or give you power over the wicked forces of the night. You must be genuinely born again to be recognized as a "terror" to the demonic kingdom.

2. Baptism of the Holy Spirit

Jesus, in Acts 1:8 says, "But you shall receive power when the Holy Spirit has come upon you…" Yes, you receive some measure of power and authority when you become born again. But there is a special and greater dimension of power and authority that comes upon you when you are baptized in the Holy Spirit.

Your Christian life in general, and your prayer life, in particular, experiences a radical transformation with the filling of the Holy Spirit. You become more energized, fervent, unyielding and dynamic in your night engagements and spiritual warfare.

To begin with, with the baptism of the Holy Spirit, you are more alert to happenings in the spiritual realm, and thus more discerning and responsive to divine promptings at night. Again, it becomes easier for you to overcome the weakness of the flesh, such that sleep will not prevail over you when you are supposed to be praying.

Additionally, the Spirit of God in you will guide you to pray aright and to pray with precision and authority. In other words, with the Holy Spirit in you, you will not be praying scattered but focused prayers; and you will not be praying with fear but with faith and authority. Also, the filling of the Holy Spirit enables you to be able to pray in the Spirit, especially speaking in tongues to convey petitions that ordinary human language will not be able to fully convey.

3. Avoiding spiritual contaminants

1 John 5:18 says, "…he that is begotten of God keepeth himself, and that wicked one toucheth him not" (KJV). What guarantees us constant victory over the devil and the powers of the night is that we keep ourselves from

all spiritual pollutants that can weaken our spirit man and render us insensitive to the promptings of the Holy Spirit or vulnerable to demonic attacks.

The number one spiritual contaminant, of course, is sin in any form. Sin comprises the works of the flesh, listed in Galatians 5:19-21 as "adultery, fornication, uncleanness, lewdness, idolatry, sorcery, hatred, contentions, jealousies, outbursts of wrath, selfish ambitions, dissensions, heresies, envy, murders, drunkenness, revelries, and the like." Sin has been rightly defined as "**S**atan's **I**dentification **N**umber" – which makes the individual his property and a lawful captive. 1 John 3:7-8 says, "Little children, let no one deceive you. He who practices righteousness is righteous, just as He is righteous. He who sins is of the devil, for the devil has sinned from the beginning…"

In Judges 16:18-20, Samson tried to rouse himself from sleep to fight his enemies, but he could not because he had been spiritually contaminated and paralyzed by the power of sin. Therefore, if you come from a background of sin or having a life of sin, I will strongly advise repentance immediately. After repentance seek to correct act of sin, as not to return to it. By so doing, you will avoid the enemy having a legal ground against you, hence your battles become easier and you can be victorious.

Apart from outright sin, however, there are other contaminants, such as demonically inspired movies, songs, books and the likes. So also are fetish objects, magical items, horoscopes, Ouija boards and consulting of false prophets, sorcerers, magicians and fortune-tellers. All of these are access routes for the powers of the night to oppress, afflict and conquer an individual. No wonder the new believers in Acts 19 did the needful, as soon as they were converted! "Also, many of those who had practiced magic brought their books together and burned them in the sight of all. And they counted up the value of them, and it totaled fifty thousand pieces of silver. So the word of the Lord grew mightily and prevailed" (Acts 19:19-20).

This is what you too must do for the word of God to prevail in your life and prayers of the night.

4. Sound knowledge of God's word

The most powerful offensive weapon you have as a believer and prayer warrior is the word of God. Ephesians 6:16-17 says, "Above all, taking the shield of faith with which you will be able to quench all the fiery darts of the wicked one. And take the helmet of salvation, and the sword of the Spirit, which is the word of God." The word of God is the sword with which you affirm your position, power, authority and immunity, as a child of God. It is the weapon with which you counter the lies of the wicked, nullify their enchantments, overturn their devices and smite all of their works.

Apart from being the sword of the Spirit, the word of God is also described as a hammer, fire and other powerful elements to show its potency in our lives and its destructive capabilities against the kingdom of darkness. This is why you must let the word of God "dwell in you richly" (Colossians 3:16). Study (not just read) the word of God daily, to understand not just your responsibilities but also your rights and privileges as a child of God. Above all, study to arm yourself with the precious promises that you have been given as a soldier of Christ. You will need these to overwrite and override every demonic handwriting and activity being plotted against you and your loved ones.

5. Solid faith and avoidance of distractions

You cannot successfully subdue the powers of the night without a solid faith in the sovereignty of God, the infallibility of His word, as well as the authority and efficacy of the name and the blood of Jesus. As you engage the powers of the night, you must understand that you are not doing it in your strength; you're doing it in the strength of the Almighty God. You are merely affirming and standing on the ground of victory that has been accomplished over 2000 years ago by the vicarious death and victorious resurrection of Jesus Christ. Colossians 2:15 says, "Having disarmed principalities and powers, He made a public spectacle of them, triumphing over them in it."

Did you see that? Principalities and powers have been disarmed already for every child of God. But you need to exercise faith in this accomplished work because the enemies will still try all manners of tricks to see whether you know your rights, position and power in Christ Jesus.

Also, in engaging the forces of the night, you must be

aware of the trick of distractions, such as feeling like there are paranormal movements, hearing strange sounds and the likes – all of which are meant to engender fear and weaken your prayer. But you must remain unmoved and unwavering in your faith. "For whatever is born of God overcomes the world. And this is the victory that has overcome the world—our faith" (1 John 5:4).

Prayer Points

1. I thank you, heavenly Father, for all the liberating and empowering truths you have revealed to me in the course of reading this book.

2. From today, I surrender my life totally to you and ask for the cleansing of the blood of Jesus in all the ways I've fallen short of your glory and expectations.

3. I receive divine grace to commit myself to the study of the Scriptures and to apply all that you show me therein.

4. I renounce all spiritual contaminants in my life and receive power to desist from them henceforth.

5. By the blood of Jesus and the victory of Calvary, I declare myself an overcomer over sin, Satan, the flesh, the world, principalities and powers, and all powers and agents of the demonic kingdom, in Jesus name.

NOTES

NOTES

NOTES

NOTES

NOTES

www.ingramcontent.com/pod-product-compliance
Lightning Source LLC
LaVergne TN
LVHW052101090426
835512LV00036B/3127